Indy Cars

BY JACK DAVID

BELLWETHER MEDIA • MINNEAPOLIS, MN

TM

Are you ready to take it to the extreme?

Torque books thrust you into the action-packed world

of sports, vehicles, and adventure. These books may

include dirt, smoke, fire, and dangerous stunts.

WARNING: READ AT YOUR OWN RISK.

This edition first published in 2008 by Bellwether Media.

No part of this publication may be reproduced in whole or in part without written permission of the publisher. For information regarding permission, write to Bellwether Media Inc., Attention: Permissions Department, Post Office Box 19349, Minneapolis, MN 55419.

Library of Congress Cataloging-in-Publication Data

David, Jack, 1968-
  Indy cars / by Jack David.
      p. cm. -- (Torque--cool rides)
  Summary: "Amazing photography accompanies engaging information about Indy cars. The combination of high-interest subject matter and light text is intended for students in grades 3 through 7"--Provided by publisher.
  Includes bibliographical references and index.
  ISBN-13: 978-1-60014-148-5 (hardcover : alk. paper)
  ISBN-10: 1-60014-148-X (hardcover : alk. paper)
  1. Indy cars--Juvenile literature. I. Title.

TL236.D3775 2008
629.228--dc22

                                                            2007040562

Contents

What Is an Indy Car?

Nothing in motor sports can match the excitement of the Indianapolis (Indy) 500. This world-famous race is packed with action. Thrilling speeds, daring passes, and frantic **pit stops** keep the fans on the edge of their seats. The cars are always the center of attention.

Indy cars are **open-wheel** race cars. The wheels sit outside the car's main body. Other racing series use similar-looking cars. Some people use the term *Indy car* to refer to any open-wheel race car. That is not correct. The only official Indy cars are the ones that race in the Indy Racing League (IRL).

7

Indy Car History

Carl Fisher built the Indianapolis Motor Speedway in 1909. His 500-mile (805-kilometer) race was soon attracting racers from across the United States. The early cars looked nothing like today's Indy cars. They were basic factory-built cars, slightly modified for racing. The modern design didn't appear until the late 1960s.

Indy cars are high-performance cars designed for racing in the IRL. The Indianapolis 500 is the league's most famous race. The IRL started in 1996. Stars such as Tony Stewart, Danica Patrick, and Sam Hornish, Jr. have made it the largest open-wheel series in the United States.

Fast FaCt

NASCAR star Tony Stewart once raced Indy cars. He won the IRL championship in 1997.

Parts of an Indy Car

Indy cars have **V8 engines**. V8 engines have eight fuel-burning **cylinders** arranged in the shape of a "V." Engines are measured in liters. An Indy car engine measures 3.5 liters (.9 gallons). This can power an Indy car to speeds greater than 200 miles (322 kilometers) per hour!

Indy cars have sleek, low-to-the-ground bodies. Carefully shaped body panels fit over the **chassis**. A large **wing** is attached to the back of the car.

The wing is like an upside-down airplane wing. Air presses it down as the Indy car moves. This pressure gives the rear wheels a better grip on the track.

K. Matsuura

K. Matsuura

Fast Fact

The IRL started the Indy Pro Series in 2002. It is a racing series in which young drivers can learn about Indy car racing.

Indy cars have smooth tires called **slicks**. Smooth tires grip paved tracks well. They also wear out quickly. Riding at 200 miles (322 kilometers) per hour with worn-out tires is very dangerous. Teams need to change the tires several times during each race.

Indy Cars in Action

The IRL's top level of racing is the Indy Car Series. Drivers in this series travel to races around the world. The biggest race of the year is the Indianapolis 500. It happens every year on the last weekend of May.

Every IRL race is filled with thrilling moments. To avoid the wind, drivers **draft** closely behind one another. Avoiding the wind lets drivers gain extra speed. Drivers risk a crash every time they make a daring pass. Their teams change tires and add fuel during lightning-quick pit stops. The pressure is always on to capture the **checkered flag** and victory.

Fast Fact

It is a tradition that the winner of the Indianapolis 500 drinks a bottle of milk after finishing the race.

Glossary

chassis–the metal tubing that forms the frame of an Indy car; the chassis supports the body of an Indy car.

checkered flag–the flag waved at the end of a race; the winner is said to "take the checkered flag."

cylinder–the part of an engine where fuel is burned; most engines have several cylinders.

draft–to closely follow another car in order to reduce wind resistance

open-wheel–a style of race car with wheels outside the body of the car

pit stop–an event during a race when a team adds fuel to the car, changes its tires, and makes adjustments or minor repairs

slicks–smooth racing tires

V8 engine–an engine with eight-fuel burning cylinders arranged in the shape of a V

wing–the part of an Indy car that sticks up in back; air pushing on the wing gives the rear tires a better grip on the race track.

To Learn More

AT THE LIBRARY

Bledsoe, Glen. *The World's Fastest Indy Cars*.
Mankato, Minn.: Capstone, 2003.

Braulick, Carrie A. *Indy Cars*.
Mankato, Minn.: Capstone, 2006.

Glaser, Jason. *Danica Patrick*.
New York: PowerKids, 2008.

ON THE WEB

Learning more about Indy cars
is as easy as 1, 2, 3.

1. Go to www.factsurfer.com

2. Enter "Indy cars" into search box.

3. Click the "Surf" button and you will
   see a list of related web sites.

With factsurfer.com, finding more information is
just a click away.

23

Index

The images in this book are reproduced through the courtesy of: Gavin Lawrence/Stringer/Getty Images, front cover, pp. 6, 14-15, 18; john j. klaiber jr, pp. 4-5; Robert Laberge/Getty Images, pp. 7, 11; Nathan Lazarnick/Getty Images, p. 9; Christ Graythen/Stringer/Getty Images, p. 10; Steve Popichak/Alamy, p. 13; Darrell Ingham/Getty Images, pp. 16, 17; Harry How/Getty Images, pp. 20-21.